TENNYSON'S TWO BROTHERS

TENNYSON'S TWO BROTHERS

The Leslie Stephen Lecture
1947

BY

HAROLD NICOLSON

CAMBRIDGE
AT THE UNIVERSITY PRESS
1947

CAMBRIDGE
UNIVERSITY PRESS

University Printing House, Cambridge CB2 8BS, United Kingdom

Published in the United States of America by Cambridge University Press, New York

Cambridge University Press is part of the University of Cambridge.

It furthers the University's mission by disseminating knowledge in the pursuit of education, learning and research at the highest international levels of excellence.

www.cambridge.org
Information on this title: www.cambridge.org/9781107647589

© Cambridge University Press 1947

First published 1947
Re-issued 2014

A catalogue record for this publication is available from the British Library

ISBN 978-1-107-64758-9 Paperback

TENNYSON'S TWO BROTHERS

I

A STRANGER, happening to ride through the village
of Somersby on a Sunday morning in 1827, would
have observed a procession crossing from the rectory
to the small thatched church across the road. At the
head of the procession stalked the rector, the Rev.
George Tennyson, gaunt, sallow, enraged. The black
blood which flowed in the veins of all the Tennysons
had in his case turned to bile. He had been disin-
herited in favour of his younger brother. The promise
of his early Cambridge days, the prospect of succeeding
to the rich estate of Bayon's Manor, had, owing to
some flicker in his father's temperament, been suddenly denied: he had been relegated to a calling for
which he had little vocation, to a small and hidden
parsonage among the Lincolnshire wolds. It is not
surprising that the Rev. George Tennyson, afflicted
as he was by one great injustice and a numerous
family, should (as his more favoured brother subsequently recorded) have 'given way to feelings arising
out of a nervous temperament'. Stern and melancholy,
he was for long remembered in the locality as being
'amazing sharp' with his children: his brooding, angry,
presence threw a shadow along the rectory walls.

Upon the rector's arm, as they walked to church,
clung his gentle and long-suffering wife, Elizabeth.
Behind them followed the regiment of their children.

The stranger, observing this procession, would have been startled by their foreign appearance. The seven lanky sons, the four lanky daughters, followed their parents in a straggling line, clasping prayer-books in their big brown hands. First came Frederick, then a Cambridge undergraduate of twenty years of age; he was accompanied by Charles, aged nineteen, and Alfred, aged eighteen; they were followed by the sequence of their younger brothers and sisters: Mary, Emily, Edward, Arthur, Septimus, Matilda, Cecilia and Horatio. Swarthy the young men were, with long loose limbs and uncombed hair; it was as if a troop of Spaniards had irrupted suddenly into the depths of rural England. When they spoke to each other, one could detect in their hollow voices, the broad vowel-sounds of the Lincolnshire dialect.

It is with Alfred Tennyson's two elder brothers, Frederick and Charles, that this lecture will be mainly concerned. The subsequent history of the eight younger children need not long detain us. I shall refer to it only as indicating the congenital talents and eccentricities of the whole Tennyson tribe. Of the four daughters, Mary, the eldest, married Judge Ker, and their son, Walter Ker, became a competent scholar and contributed several volumes to the Loeb Classical Library. Cecilia married Edmund Lushington, of Park House, Maidstone, the scene of the Prologue to the *Princess*. Emily, having been engaged to Arthur Hallam, subsequently married Captain Richard Jesse of the Royal Navy. In her declining years she became a Swedenborgian and a spiritualist.

And Matilda, who was referred to by the family as 'Tilly' developed religious melancholia and would sit for hours beside the fire sobbing over the eternal damnation of her kith and kin: she died in 1913 in her hundredth year.

Of the four younger sons there is little to record; it does not seem that their subsequent relations with their famous brother were either intimate or constant. In Burke's *Peerage* for 1890 (the proof of which must surely have been revised either by the Laureate or his son), no information is provided about them, beyond their dates of birth. Edward, who once published a sonnet in the *Yorkshire Literary Annual* was for many years kept in confinement and lived until 1890. Arthur was twice married and resided at Hampstead. Horatio, unlike the rest of the family, displayed no literary tastes whatsoever; he is reported by his nephew never to have opened a book; he desired to enter the army but was packed off to Tasmania; he married Charlotte Carey Elwes and had three children. Septimus incurred the Laureate's displeasure by mooning about the lanes of County Down dressed in a long black cape with a huge sombrero on his head. Of him is told a story which his great-niece, Miss Tennyson Jesse, assures me is authentic. Some guests, arriving early for a dinner party, were startled by a huge black man who unrolled himself slowly from the hearth rug. 'I am Septimus', he said, 'the most morbid of all the Tennysons.' There remain the two elder brothers, Frederick and Charles. About them we have much more information.

II

I have heard a story that on one occasion the Laureate was asked by a daring visitor what poetry had most influenced him in his youth. 'My own', Lord Tennyson is said to have replied, 'at the age of five.' There is no doubt that the three elder sons of the Rev. George Tennyson, Frederick, Charles and Alfred, composed verses together from their earliest years. They shared a bedroom in the rectory attic which was approached by a dark staircase from the ground floor and which possessed, in addition to the small lattice window, a skylight which has since been closed up. This room is celebrated in one of the more unfortunate of the Laureate's early poems:

> Oh darling room, my heart's delight,
> Dear room, the apple of my sight,
> With thy two couches [there were in
>   fact three couches] soft and white,
>
> There is no room so exquisite,
> No little room so warm and bright
> Wherein to read, wherein to write.

This poem (which Arthur Hallam had, with his usual impulsive adulation, pronounced to be 'mighty pleasant') was included in the 1830 volume and exposed the young Tennyson to Lockhart's scathing derision and to Bulwer's gibe about 'schoolmiss Alfred'. A later critic referred to Somersby in general, and to the attic bedroom in particular, as 'a nest of singing birds'. And it was certainly in the darling room that Alfred Tennyson, urged on by the example and encouragement of his two elder brothers, composed his earliest poems.

The result of this triple activity was a volume entitled *Poems by Two Brothers*. This volume, the manuscript of which can be seen in Trinity College Library, was published by J. and J. Jackson of Louth in the last months of 1826, although it bears the imprint of 1827. All three brothers contributed to the volume; it contains forty-eight poems by Alfred, forty-eight poems by Charles, and three by Frederick, including a long and meaningless rhapsody entitled *The Oak of the North.*

When shown this forgotten volume in his later years, the Laureate expressed astonishment at its excellent quality. He was annoyed, however, by the statement that the poems had been written when the authors were between fifteen and eighteen years of age. 'I myself', he wrote, 'had at the time done far better things. When these poems were published, Charles was eighteen. I was seventeen.'

It is seldom profitable to dissect juvenilia, nor can it be said that this collection of 1826 displays any marked precocity. Yet the volume is interesting as showing us—by its innumerable quotations, footnotes and epigraphs—what a wide and unorthodox range of books the Rev. George Tennyson allowed his sons to read.

There are twenty quotations from Horace, eight from Virgil, six from Byron, five from Isaiah, four from Ossian, three from Cicero, and two each from Moore, Xenophon, Milton, Claudian and Jeremiah.

In addition, we have references to such varied writers as John Clare, Juvenal, Gibbon, Young, Appolonius Rhodius, Lucretius, Rousseau, Chapman, Spenser and Shakespeare. Frederick, it is true, had been at Eton and was at the time an undergraduate at St John's College, from which he was later transferred to Trinity. But Charles and Alfred, after a miserable period at the grammar school at Louth, had been educated at home; it was in their father's study that they absorbed such scholarship as they possessed. Their reading may not perhaps have been very deep; it was certainly both varied and wide.

It is curious, moreover, to examine the poems attributed to each of the three brothers and to note both the similarities and the differences. One finds, for instance, a common love of domesticity, a common preoccupation with detail, and a common absence of even the rudiments of humour. 'Oh! never', exclaims Charles Tennyson:

> Oh! never may frowns and dissension molest
>   The pleasure I find at the social hearth;
> A pleasure the dearest—the purest—the best
>   Of all that are found or enjoy'd on the earth!

Those lines, if technically better modulated, could well have been written by Alfred Tennyson in the earlier—or indeed in the later—stages of his development. The note of domesticity, the rectory parlour note, or what his enemies would call the 'schoolmiss Alfred note', was apt to recur even in the poems of his maturity. He would himself have defended and described such passages as 'tender passages'. 'Where's now', he writes at the age of sixteen or seventeen:

> Where's now that peace of mind
>   O'er youth's pure bosom stealing,
> So sweet and so refin'd,
>   So exquisite a feeling?

Such verses may be crude; but the sentiment, the sensitiveness, recur.

In seeking to deduce from *Poems by Two Brothers* the atmosphere of Somersby rectory, we notice also a foretaste of the Laureate's minute observation of nature, of his preoccupation with detail. In a contribution by Charles Tennyson we find the lines:

> The smallest herb or leaf can charm
> The man whom nature's beauties warm.

And here is one of Alfred Tennyson's stanzas, which (humourless and clumsy though it be) does certainly foreshadow something of his later energy of perception:

> The glittering fly, the wondrous things
>   That microscopic art descries;
> The lion of the waste which springs
>   Bounding upon his enemies;
> The mighty sea-snake of the storm,
> The vorticella's viewless form.

It is characteristic of Alfred Tennyson's unfortunate habits of precision that the word 'vorticella' is explained in a footnote. 'See', we are reminded, 'Baker on Animalculae.'

More important than these similarities are the differences which one can observe in the earliest poems of these three brothers. In Frederick's verses we

11

notice that addiction to rhetoric which, although almost wholly meaningless, impressed Edward Fitzgerald profoundly. We also notice his uncertain handling of vowel sounds and grammar. Frederick opens one of his three contributions as follows:

> 'Tis the voice of the dead
>   From the depths of their glooms:
> Hark! they call me away
>   To the world of the tombs.

Fitzgerald, it seems, enjoyed that sort of thing. He called it: 'Such gloomy grand stuff as you write.'

In Charles' poems we notice the timid appreciation of small and delicate things. He writes of 'the pensile dew-drop's twinkling gleam', of thistle-down, of glow-worms. In all his later poetry we find the themes of dew and gossamer invariably recurring. And in Alfred's poems we are impressed, not merely by a metrical power far more compelling than that of his two elder brothers, not merely by his precocious aptitude in the combination of vowel-sounds, but also by a note of that gloomy mysticism which in after years produced his finest poetry. Neither Charles nor Frederick was capable of writing a stanza such as this which Alfred composed before he was seventeen:

> I wander in darkness and sorrow,
>   Unfriended and cold and alone,
> As dismally gurgles beside me
>   The bleak river's desolate moan,
> The rise of the volleying thunder
>   The mountain's low echoes repeat;
> The roar of the wind is around me,
>   The leaves of the year at my feet.

Yet this lecture, I repeat, is not directly concerned with Alfred Tennyson; it is concerned with Frederick and Charles. And since, with the publication of *Poems by Two Brothers*, the three part company, I must now leave the attic bedroom of Somersby and speak, first about Frederick and thereafter about Charles: about Tennyson's two brothers.

III

There are few pastimes more agreeable than that of strolling through the byways of literature. True it is that one is obliged to traverse many arid patches and much sandy waste; but from time to time one discovers little coppices of loveliness or some strange quirk of nature which arouses interest or surprise. Of these small surprises one of the most constant is that caused by the inability, even of gifted men and women, properly to estimate the relative value of their contemporaries. Edward Fitzgerald, for instance, was a man of wide culture, sensitive literary taste and considerable critical acumen. He was one of the first to recognize and expound the genius of Blake. But when it came to balancing the merits of the three Tennyson brothers his judgement became strangely uncertain. I am not suggesting of course that Fitzgerald was unaware that Charles was a better poet than Frederick and Alfred a better poet than either. All I am suggesting is that Fitzgerald did not assess correctly the relative value of the three brothers or realize with sufficient clarity that, whereas Alfred Tennyson was among the great poets of all time, and whereas Charles Tennyson was a minor English poet of some distinction, Frederick Tennyson was little more than a rather boring eccentric with a knack of writing verse.

Fitzgerald did not know the Tennyson brothers during the Cambridge period, although he remembered seeing Alfred Tennyson at Trinity and described him as 'a sort of Hyperion'. Their friendship dates from the time when they had all four left the University. I have a suspicion that Alfred Tennyson, dominated as he was by Arthur Hallam and his fellow apostles, did not take Frederick's odd friend too seriously and may even have treated him with patronizing disdain. Since although Fitzgerald in his letters often refers to 'dear old Alfred', yet he also remarks that he was 'very droll and very wayward', and that 'he writes the names of his friends in water'. Twice every year throughout his life Fitzgerald would send an amicable letter to Farringford or Aldworth; but these letters were answered, not by the Laureate, but by Lady Tennyson or her son. It may have been the chill occasioned thereby to Fitzgerald's over-warm affections that induced him to underestimate the Laureate's later poems and to attribute to those of Frederick and Charles a comparative value which they did not in fact possess. To him, Alfred Tennyson was 'a man of genius who, I think, has crippled his growth by over-elaboration'. He frequently expressed the regret that Alfred had published anything after the 1842 volume. He condemned

The Princess as 'a wretched waste of power' and contended that the songs in that poem (which we rightly regard as among the loveliest of all English lyrics) lacked 'the old champagne flavour'. He disliked *In Memoriam*. 'What can it do', he asked, 'but make us all sentimental?' 'I almost', he confessed, 'feel hopeless about Alfred now.'

Such errors of judgement should prepare us for Fitzgerald's curious overestimation of Frederick Tennyson's verse. He had a deep admiration for what he called Frederick's 'energetic, stirring, acquisitive and capacious soul'. He liked him for being 'strong, haughty and passionate'. His poetry appeared to be inspired by 'strong and genuine imagination'. It contained, so Fitzgerald asserted, 'heaps of single lines, couplets and stanzas which could consume all the Xs and Ys like stubble'. The only criticism he would permit himself was on the score of prolixity. 'A little', he wrote, 'of the vulgar faculty of popular tact is all that needs to be added to you.' 'Old Fred', he confessed many years later to Fanny Kemble, 'might have been one of the Three Brothers could he have compressed himself into something of the Sonnet compass; but he couldn't.' How far were these eulogies and these criticisms justified? Let me first examine the life and work of Frederick Tennyson.

IV

Frederick Tennyson, the eldest surviving son of the
Rev. George Tennyson, was born in June 1807 and
died in 1898 at the age of ninety-one. Unlike the
other Tennysons, he possessed a fair complexion and
blue eyes; his hair was scraped back from his forehead
and fell in girlish ringlets down his back; there are
those still living who can recall a huge domed forehead and this strange falling cluster of silver curls.
At Eton, although good at cricket and Captain of the
Oppidans, he was remembered mainly for his lack of
social gifts. 'Rather a silent, solitary boy', records
Sir Francis Doyle, 'not always in perfect harmony
with Keate.' This inability to adjust himself to his
surroundings remained with him throughout his life.
He described himself later as 'a person of gloomy
insignificance and unsocial monomania'. He had a
special loathing of what was then the aristocracy. He
derided what he called 'the high jinks of the high
nosed, who go about with well cut trousers and ill-
arranged ideas'. Frederick's own clothes were Italian
rather than well cut; nor can it be said that his ideas
were ever well arranged.

He left Eton in 1827 and went first to his father's
old college of St John's and subsequently to Trinity,
where he was later joined by Charles and Alfred. He
obtained a Browne Medal for a Sapphic ode upon the
Pyramids, but when he graduated in 1832 it was without distinction. It was originally intended that he
should enter the Church, but this suggestion filled

him with acute alarm. In 1833 he inherited a property near Grimsby and immediately left England for the Mediterranean. He remained absent for twenty-six years.

There is little of interest to record of Frederick Tennyson's long and self-imposed exile. For a time he lived in the island of Corfu, where a cousin was secretary to the High Commissioner. He thereafter migrated to Italy where he married Maria Giuliotti, daughter of the chief magistrate of Siena. We hear of him in 1841, playing a game of cricket at Naples with the officers of the *Bellerephon* and beating them by ninety runs. We hear of him later in Florence where he rented the Villa Gondi, and later the Villa Torrigiani. The main room in the latter residence had been decorated by Michael Angelo. Frederick was devoted to music and would sit for hours in this magnificent room while fiddlers played to him the compositions of Mozart. 'I am a regular family man', he wrote, 'with four children (the last of whom promises to be the most eccentric of a humorous set) and an umbrella.' And then in 1853, when he was forty-six years of age, an event occurred which altered the course of his life. He met the Brownings.

Browning [he wrote] is a wonderful man with inexhaustible memory, animal spirits and bonhomie.... Mrs B. never goes out—being troubled like other inspired ladies with a chest—is a little unpretending woman, yet full of power, and, what is far better, loving-kindness; and never so happy as when she can get into the thick of mysterious Clairvoyants, Rappists, Ecstatics, and Swedenborgians.

17

This meeting had two important results. Browning persuaded him to print his poetry. Mrs Browning introduced him to spiritualism.

Frederick Tennyson's first volume was published in 1854 when he was forty-seven and was called *Days and Hours*. The choice of that title had evidently been suggested to him by the opening words of section 117 of *In Memoriam*. The book was not ill received. 'The poems', wrote Charles Kingsley, 'are the work of a finished scholar, of a man who knows all schools, who has profited more or less by all, and who can often express himself, while revelling in luxurious fancies, with a grace and terseness which Pope himself might have envied.' The word 'terseness' is the last word which I should myself apply to the poetry of Frederick Tennyson; other critics were less amiable than Charles Kingsley; and Frederick, being just as sensitive to adverse criticism as were his two brothers, remained silent thereafter for a space of thirty-six years.

In 1857 he left Italy and bought a house in Jersey overlooking St Heliers. He remained there for forty years. In 1880 his wife died; in 1890 at the age of eighty-three he published his second volume of poetry, *The Isles of Greece*; in 1891 *Daphne* appeared; and in 1895 *Poems of the Day and the Year*. He died in his son's house in Kensington in February 1898. Such was the uneventful and somewhat feckless life of Frederick Tennyson.

Before I examine the nature of his poetic inspiration, I must consider for a moment the effect upon his mind and character of the Swedenborgian doctrines to which he was introduced by Mrs Browning. He had begun with the more ordinary exercises in spiritualism, with clairvoyants, with table-rapping and with automatic writing. Before long, however, he found these manifestations insufficient; he indulged in wider experiments. He became convinced that the spirits were seeking to enter into direct personal communication with him by means of electrical tickings in the air. With desperate application he sought to interpret to himself the meaning of these morse messages. He was pleased and flattered when a medium disclosed that he saw Frederick constantly and closely accompanied by the ghost of Mozart. He was convinced that the millenium was approaching when there would be no further barriers between the invisible and the visible world. In 1872 he came into contact with a certain Mr Melville who assured him that he had discovered a forgotten system for reading the stars which would provide a new explanation of the masonic signs and symbols. He accompanied Mr Melville to England and sought to convince the Grand Master of the importance of this discovery. It was then that Fitzgerald saw him for the last time. 'Quite grand', he wrote to Fanny Kemble, 'and sincere in this as in all else; with the Faith of a gigantic child, pathetic and yet humorous to consider and consort with.' That chance meeting with Mrs Browning had produced a permanent effect. 'The supernatural', wrote Frederick Tennyson, 'has occupied and absorbed my whole soul to the exclusion of almost every subject which the Gorillas of this world most delight in, whether scientific, political or literary.' It has been said that in his

19

later years his faith in spiritualism suffered a decline. Yet in 1887 when the Laureate visited him at St Heliers he begged his famous brother to abandon poetry for ever and to devote what years remained to him of life to the study and propagation of the gospel of Swedenborg. From all of which it may appear to you that Frederick Tennyson, at least in the second half of his life, was a most eccentric man. And what about his poetry?

<h2 style="text-align:center">V</h2>

It is not my intention to weary you with the poems which Frederick Tennyson published after he was eighty years of age. The *Isles of Greece* is a long rhythmical romance, written in clumsy blank verse, the main feature of which is an imaginary love affair between Sappho and Alcaeus. In this story Atthis is made to appear as a child of two and Anaktoria as a merchant princess. *Daphne and other Poems* is equally long-winded, meaningless and ill composed. From time to time one catches a faint echo of the Laureate's mighty rhythm, but in fact, Frederick did not possess a delicate ear for blank verse, even as he did not possess much power of observation. It is a curious fact that although he, unlike Alfred, had actually visited the Greek islands, he is totally unable to convey the Hellenic atmosphere. Alfred, who had never been to the Aegean, could write:

> For now the noonday quiet holds the hill:
> The grasshopper is silent in the grass;
> The lizard with his shadow on the stone,
> Rests like a shadow, and the winds are dead.

But Frederick who had spent almost a year in the Greek islands could introduce into a description of Mitylene the line 'Green plots alive with songs of happy birds'. Which suggests that he never noticed anything at all. Were these his only publications, then the name of Frederick Tennyson would not need to be recorded among our English poets. He would be of interest only as a pale reflection of his glorious brother, a reflection as pallid as the faint glow of a gibbous moon through the mist. His first volume, *Days and Hours*, does, however, deserve serious consideration, if only because it shows us how deep and lasting was the impress left upon the three brothers by the contrast between their own unhappy nerves and the protective assurances of Somersby.

There are, of course, certain passages in *Days and Hours* which are peculiar to Frederick himself. His colours are deeper and at times more violent than those used by either of his two brothers; the word 'purple' occurs with wearisome iteration; and the grapes and vine-leaves of Italy entwine themselves across almost every page. His natural irritability, which was more vivacious than either the neurasthenia of Charles or the black moods of Alfred, is often apparent. It echoes in a striking poem entitled *The First of March*:

> Larks twitter, martens glance, and curs from afar
>   Rage down the wind, and straight are heard no
>   more;
>   Old wives creep out and scold and bang the door;
> And clanging clocks grow angry in the air.

We hear his 'unsocial monomania' in the couplet:

> And when the proud world, tyrannous and strong,
> Tramples frail hearts into the dust of scorn.

This sentiment is echoed in one of the few outstanding lines in the *Isles of Greece* when he rails at the elegant with the words:

> Your thoughts
> Are harsh and boastful as the peacock's cry.

And then, of course, we have the special diffuseness, the meaningless prolixity, which render most of Frederick's poems so wearisome to read. One's patience none the less is rewarded by sudden echoes of the authentic note of Somersby. We meet the Brook again, that simple little stream which fringed the rectory garden and by which all three of the Tennysons were so lastingly impressed. The flower beds, the pleached walk, even the lawn are mentioned. Strange, indeed, that twenty-six years later the memory of this ageing man should revert to the home which he had known in boyhood; that he should write of the church clock and of the benches under the porch; and that the sounds of Lincolnshire should come back to him so vividly among the violins and frescoes of his Florentine saloons:

> On the high wold, the last look of the sun
>   Burns like a beacon, over dale and stream;
> The shouts have ceased, the laughter and the fun;
>   The Grandma sleeps and peaceful be her dream;
> Only a hammer on an anvil rings;
>   The day is dying—still the blackbird sings.

More interesting even than these sudden nostalgic glimpses is that sense of spiritual loneliness, of twilight fear, which haunts many of the finest poems which his great brother wrote. Frederick also could hear these 'prophetic voices low'; he also was attuned to:

> Dim thoughts, that reach us from the Infinite
> Faint as far seas, or twilight in eclipse;

he also could:

> see from off Time's dim gray shore
> The sunken tide of the world's blessed years.

He also could feel himself abandoned upon a moonless plain, and he also could be stirred almost to major poetry by the mystery of the half-light which comes before the dawn:

> Just then, 'tween Day and Night,
> I heard a wild bird singing in the dawn
> Far over hill, and stream, and wood and lawn
> That solitary magic took its flight,
> That holy, tender utterance of delight,
> By loving echoes deep into the forest drawn.

VI

In the second section of this lecture I described how the three Tennyson boys composed their earliest poems together in the intensive domesticity of their attic bedroom. In the fifth section I have tried to show how Frederick Tennyson, living all those years in

Italy and sundered from his two brothers in mind and spirit, was only able to rise above the middle levels of his talents when visited by memories of Somersby, or when haunted by that twilight fear which flickers like some marsh-light above the swamps of Tennysonian gloom. In the concluding sections I shall consider the life and work of the second of the three brothers, Charles.

If there be any purpose in this triple confrontation it is to enable you for a short space to view one of the greatest of our English poets from an unaccustomed angle. Here you have three brothers, inheriting a similar neurotic disposition, bred and educated in almost identical circumstances, sharing the same boyhood associations, and all endowed with a certain creative faculty. Each of these three brothers wrote poetry over a space of more than fifty years; to each of them the contrast between the security of Somersby and the harsh clangour of the outside world remained a recurrent source of inspiration; but whereas Frederick wrote a few pretty stanzas, and whereas Charles composed a number of admirable sonnets, Alfred had the power to cause these simple rectory tunes to wail and thunder and resound...which indicates that genius is not a matter of environment but derives from the fortuitous combination of certain hidden cells.

There is little to record of the placid life of Charles Tennyson. He was a year older than Alfred and shared with him the miseries of Louth grammar school, the domestic education of Somersby, and the rigours of their father's irritable temperament. The two brothers matriculated at Trinity on the same day in February 1828. Charles won a Bell scholarship, graduated in 1832, and three years later became vicar of Grasby, a small hamlet in his native Lincolnshire. In 1836 he married Louisa Sellwood, whose younger sister became in later years the Laureate's devoted and admiring wife. In 1837 he inherited a property from his great-uncle Samuel Turner of Caistor and assumed the additional surname of Turner; it was as Charles Tennyson-Turner that he was thereafter known. He devoted his whole life to the needs of his small and backward parish; he rebuilt the vicarage and restored the church and the school; he was without children and interested himself in the composition of sonnets, the study of Italian, and the minute observation of nature. He died in April 1879, at the age of seventy-one.

In spite of this placid and seemingly unruffled existence, Charles had full share of the family neurosis and eccentricity. Shortly after his marriage he suffered a complete nervous breakdown and for a space of time he had to be segregated from all contact with the outer world. His appearance was strange indeed; his swarthy face was framed in long untidy ringlets; although as unkempt as the the rest of the Tennysons, he took particular trouble about his clothes; the cuffs of his shirt were turned back over his coat sleeves in the manner of Count d'Orsay; he shared with Septimus, Alfred and Arthur, a liking for enormous black capes and large sombreros. His voice was gruff and deep; it was in his intonation, and in that of his sister Emily, that the Lincolnshire accent was most noticeable. When confronted with strangers he would actually tremble with fear. After a short period of estrangement in the early years of their marriage, his wife, who would refer to him as 'Cubbie', watched over him with selfless devotion. Three weeks after his death she followed him to the grave.

Although the Laureate did not possess or preserve any deep family affections, there is no doubt that Charles was closer to him than any other of his brothers and sisters. When staggering under the shock of Arthur Hallam's death, Alfred had written section nine of *In Memoriam* which contains the following wounding stanza:

> My Arthur, whom I shall not see
> Till all my widow'd race be run;
> Dear as the mother to the son,
> More than my brothers are to me.

It may have been this stanza which, when *In Memoriam* was first published anonymously, induced a reviewer to remark that 'these verses have evidently been composed by the widow of a military man'. In any case the stanza caused offence to Charles Tennyson-Turner. One would have supposed that, on learning this, Alfred would have excluded the offending passage from the published edition. He did nothing of the sort. He merely added section seventy-nine; and we are glad that he did so, since it provides

us with a valuable statement of the contrasting appeal
of Somersby and Arthur Hallam:

'More than my brothers are to me'—
   Let this not vex thee noble heart!
   I know thee of what force thou art
To hold the costliest love in fee.

But thou and I are one in kind,
   As moulded like in Nature's mint;
   And hill and wood and field did print
The same sweet forms in either mind.

For us the same cold streamlet curl'd
   Thro' all its eddying coves; the same
   All winds that roam the twilight came
In whispers of the beauteous world.

At one dear knee we proferred vows
   One lesson from one book we learn'd
   Ere childhood's flaxen ringlet turned
To black and brown on kindred brows.

And so my wealth resembles thine,
   But he was rich where I was poor,
   And he supplied my want the more
As his unlikeness fitted mine.

When many years afterwards the news of Charles's
death reached Farringford the Laureate composed a
commemorative poem entitled *Midnight June 20
1879*. It is not a successful ode, since the poet's
attention was distracted from his grief at the death
of a beloved brother, by his fury at the vagaries of the
British climate. There is far too much about the
'cuckoo of a joyless June' being succeeded by 'the

cuckoo of a worse July'. But it does contain two stanzas which are worth quotation:

> And thro' this midnight breaks the sun
>   Of sixty years away,
> The light of days when life begun,
>   The days that seem to-day.
>
> When all my griefs were shared with thee
>   And all my hopes were thine—
> As all thou wert was one with me,
>   May all thou art be mine.

VII

The intimate association between Charles and Alfred during their early youth is signalized by the fact that they each produced their first independent volume of poetry in the same year. In March 1830 Charles published in Cambridge a volume entitled *Sonnets and Fugitive Pieces*. In June 1830 Alfred published with Effingham Wilson in London *Poems Chiefly Lyrical*, thereafter to be known as the '1830 volume'. The two books were sent by the kindly Arthur Hallam with a covering note to Leigh Hunt, who was then editing *The Tatler*. Hallam forestalled Leigh Hunt's probable criticism by suggesting that the poems by the two Tennyson brothers might not appeal to the common reader but 'only to the elect church of Urania, which we know to be small and in tribulation'. Leigh Hunt responded immediately. He devoted four successive reviews in *The Tatler* to an examination of Charles's sonnets and Alfred's lyrics. 'We have had great pleasure', he wrote, 'in stating that we have seen no such poetical writing since the last volume of Mr Keats; and that the authors, who are both young men, we believe at College, may take their stand at once among the first poets of the day.' It is interesting to record that at the time Leigh Hunt believed that Charles showed the greater promise of the two. He was, however, too experienced a critic not to detect a certain absence of energy in Charles's compositions. 'I was fearful', he wrote later, 'of what he would come to, by certain misgivings in his poetry and a want of active poetic faith.'

Even more curious was the impression made by Charles's first volume of sonnets upon Wordsworth, who was visiting Cambridge at the time. 'We have', he wrote in November 1830, 'a respectable show of blossom in poetry—two brothers of the name of Tennyson, one in particular not a little promising.' We might have assumed from this remark that Wordsworth had noticed that Alfred possessed genius, whereas Charles was gifted only with a delicate talent. But it was not so. When Emerson visited Rydal Mount in 1848 Wordsworth remarked to him 'that he had thought an elder brother of Tennyson at first the better poet, but must now reckon Alfred the true one'.

Coleridge also was much impressed by Charles's first volume. 'The old man at Highgate', wrote Arthur Hallam to Emily Tennyson, 'has rejoiced over him.' This rejoicing, however, was not entirely uncritical. There exists in the British Museum a copy of this 1830 edition of Charles's sonnets with annotations in Coleridge's hand. It is true that he dubbed the sonnet *To a Lark* as 'one of the finest in the language'; it is true that he scribbled the more general comment that Charles Tennyson 'stood between Wordsworth and Southey partaking of the excellencies of both'. But he was too acute not to observe the absence of any compelling poetic force. 'The feeling', he annotates at one moment, 'seems to me fluttering and unsteady, pouncing and skimming on a succession of truisms.'

The Laureate himself would always maintain in later years that Charles's sonnets had 'all the tenderness of the Greek epigram'. 'I sometimes think', he said to Canon Rawnsley, 'that of their kind, there is nothing equal to them in English poetry.' 'I at least', he said again, 'rank my brother's sonnets next to those of the three Olympians'—Shakespeare, Milton and Wordsworth. This view was shared by Sir Henry Taylor. 'There are none', he wrote, 'in the language more beautiful in their sincerity and truth.' Only the Brownings maintained the startling opinion that Frederick Tennyson was a greater poet.

How much of this contemporary adulation can be accepted to-day? A more modern critic has, in my opinion, struck a happier balance. 'The sonnets of Charles Tennyson-Turner', he writes, 'live because their freshness conquers an almost unparalleled technical casualness.' It is on this more moderate note that I propose to examine in conclusion the poetry of Charles Tennyson.

VIII

After publication in 1830 of his first volume of poetry,
Charles Tennyson was afflicted with one of those prolonged silences which were apt to descend on all the
Tennysons. For thirty-four years he remained dumb
and it was not till 1864 that he again ventured into
print. The collection of sonnets published in that year
was followed by two further collections in 1868 and
1873; after his death the whole of his work was
issued under the title *Collected Sonnets, Old and
New*, with a biographical memoir by his nephew
Hallam Tennyson and a critical appreciation by James
Spedding.

It may have been that his prolonged silence was
occasioned by ill-health or that he felt himself over-
shadowed by his illustrious younger brother. Charles
Tennyson-Turner was more than a diffident man; he
was almost morbidly modest. He became obsessed
with the conviction that he possessed no original
talent whatsoever and that his sonnets were no more
than imitations and recollections of the work of others.
Even robust writers can be afflicted with this obses-
sion; it is a price paid for extreme and oversensitive
intellectual integrity. Leslie Stephen, to whose
memory this lecture is dedicated, was one of the most
healthy minded of all our men of letters; yet even he
could be assailed by doubts regarding his own authen-
ticity. 'I always suffer', he wrote to Croom Robert-
son, 'from a latent conviction that I am an impostor
and that somebody will find me out.' Charles

Tennyson was no more of an impostor than was Leslie Stephen; yet with him diffidence developed almost into a disease. He never realized that he was a true poet, whose talents, although restricted, were original, delicate, sincere, and above all refreshingly spontaneous. And his life was clouded by long dark periods when he became convinced that such inspiration as he possessed had deserted him for ever:

> The edge of thought was blunted by the stress
> Of the hard world; my fancy had wax'd dull,
> All nature seem'd less nobly beautiful—
> Robbed of her grandeur and her loveliness;
> Methought the Muse within my heart had died.

Nor did he ever believe, as Frederick sometimes believed, that his Muse, even when present to him, could compete with his great brother's mightier resonance:

> But still I may misuse some honest theme,
> Tinkling this idle outgrowth of my brain;
> A hair amid the harpstrings! My weak words
> May pass unheard among the rolling chords.

The modesty of Charles's pretension—so different from Frederick's ambitious diffuseness—served him well. He would have failed miserably had he attempted to write on the grand scale; where he succeeded was in the delicate restricted and sensitive rendering of small observed incidents. The sonnet entitled *Letty's Globe* is familiar to us from the anthologies; it is not —to my mind—the best of Charles's poems. He possessed an original and charming capacity for identifying himself with tiny things. "O Thou' he wrote:

> Oh Thou, who givest to the woodland wren
> A throat, like to a little light-set door
> That opens to his early joy. . . .

His sympathies were instantaneous; let me read to you a sonnet which he wrote when on a holiday in Wales on seeing the cattle trucks pass down the line from Holyhead to London.

> My open window overlooked the rails,
> When suddenly, a cattle train went by,
> Rapt, in a moment from my pitying eye,
> As from their lowing mates in Irish vales;
> Close-pack'd and mute they stood, as close as bees,
> Bewildered with their fright and narrow room;
> 'Twas sad to see that meek-eyed hecatomb,
> So fiercely hurried past our summer seas,
> Our happy bathers and our fresh sea-breeze,
> And hills of blooming heather, to their doom.

This gift of rapid sympathy extends even to inanimate objects; Charles enjoyed writing tender sonnets upon such things as abandoned rocking horses, buoy-bells, a canary's empty cage, scarecrows and even hydraulic rams. Delicate was his touch, even fragile, as light and quick as 'the morning beam along the gossamer'. His sonnets suffer, however, from a curious clumsiness of diction; neither he nor Frederick possessed their brother's amazing sensitiveness to sounds. The following sonnet, entitled *The Lattice at Sunrise*, conveys the charm as well as the ungainliness of Charles's manner:

> As on my bed at dawn I mus'd and pray'd,
> I saw my lattice prankt upon the wall,
> The flaunting leaves and flitting birds withal—
> A sunny phantom interlaced with shade;
> 'Thanks be to heaven', in happy mood I said,
> 'What sweeter aid my matins could befall
> Than this fair glory from the East hath made?
> What holy sleights hath God, the Lord of all,
> To bid us feel and see! we are not free
> To say we see not, for the glory comes
> Nightly and daily, like the flowing sea;
> His lustre pierceth through the midnight glooms
> And, at prime hour, behold! He follows me
> With golden shadows to my secret rooms!'

One cannot imagine Alfred Tennyson permitting himself those ugly internal assonances of 'see' and 'free' and 'feel'. And yet the poem does contain something of Charles's fleeting sunbeam delicacy.

I have begun by indicating those aspects of Charles Tennyson's poetic talent which differentiated him from his elder and his younger brother. I must conclude on a more Tennysonian note. We have Somersby again, with its familiar domestic atmosphere, coming with that tug at the heart which assailed all the Tennysons when they recalled their boyhood years. 'And from the grove', writes Charles Tennyson:

> And from the grove which skirts this garden glade
> I had my earliest thoughts of love and spring.

And finally, we have that curious flickering loneliness which one finds in the better poems of Frederick, and which suggested again and again to Alfred some of his most immortal lines. For underneath the sentimental gentleness of Charles's poetry, detached from the delicate radiance of the world he loved, there brooded what he called 'the dark twilight of an autumn dawn'. It is this almost mystic sense of loneliness which echoes in the lines which Coleridge so much admired:

> Disordered music, deep and tear-compelling,
> Like siren voices pealing o'er the seas.

It is this which colours the fine sonnet called *A Forest Lake* with its concluding chords:

> Or when cool eve is busy on thy shores,
> With trails of purple shadow from the West,
> Or dusking in the wake of tardy oars.

And it is this which inspired the haunting lines:

> I'd bid that crumbled mound from Babylon
> Come looming up at sundown, with the moan
> Of evening winds. . . .

It would indeed be foolish to contend that either of Alfred Tennyson's two brothers can rank among our major poets. Frederick was too wild, too eccentric, too diffuse: Charles too limited and too evanescent. But each of them serves to throw some light upon the complicated temperament of their younger brother; and to help us better to understand the jangled nerves, the brooding melancholy, the spiritual loneliness of that sensitive mystic; and the grandeur of the poetry that he wrote.